Garage Sale *Magic!*

How to turn your 'trash' into cash!

Simply & Easily!

ACKNOWLEDGEMENTS

With the knowledge that we have obtained by conducting dozens of
GARAGE SALES for ourselves and our friends; thanks must go to our
family for all of their help in assisting us with our garage sales; our
neighbors who have had to put up with the crowds, parking and
additional traffic, and the garage sale 'junkies', who continue to teach
us about negotiation and value.

International Standard Book Number: 0-9638152-0-2
Library of Congress Catalog Card Number: 93-72562
Printed in the United States of America

Book Cover and Illustrations by Christopher J. Burlini
DeFrancesco Gallery

Garage
Sale
Magic!

by Michael & Pam Williams

Freedom Publishing Co.
400 West Dundee Road
Buffalo Grove, Il. 60089

If you can't get people to listen
to you any other way,
tell them it's confidential.

Farmer's Digest

TABLE OF CONTENTS

There are some people
that if they don't know,
you can't tell 'em.

Louis Armstrong

GARAGE SALE MAGIC!

By Michael and Pam Williams

INTRODUCTION

Although we have been going to, and preparing garage sales for almost twenty years, it is *amazing* to us how few people take advantage of garage sales! There are so many reasons for you to have a garage sale, and so very few reasons why you shouldn't! We have our own garage sale each year, from which we generate at least $2,500 per garage sale! Yes, you read it right! *We have never generated less than $2,500 at our own garage sale!*

Although money is a very important factor, it is not the only purpose to hold a garage sale. During the course of a year (especially if you have a family with children, as we do), you will generate a tremendous amount of storage, piles and yes, junk! If you haven't had a garage sale in a while, it is difficult to describe to you the exhilaration that is felt when you have gotten rid of all that stuff! Not only do you have fewer piles, emptier closets and storage bins, but your house breathes a sigh of relief, saying "thank you!". In other words, by getting rid of volumes of 'junk', you are effectively *expanding* your home, since it will be able to store more 'stuff' that comes along in the next year.

Yes, money is also important!

With the annual proceeds from our garage sales, you can...

> *...fixed up the house,*
> *...gotten new landscaping,*
> *...replaced our appliances (refrigerator, washer/dryer, etc.*
> *...bought a new, big screen color t.v.,*
> *...taken many summer vacations,*
> *...used the money as a down payment for a new car, and*
> *...yes, even gotten a new garage!*

Over all, you can have a lot of fun with garage sales, and we would like to give you some helpful hints, creative ideas, and do's and don'ts that will help you to...

Maximize your garage sale profits!

In the next few pages, we will discuss with you such

important items as:

Why are garage sales so popular?
What to sell
Where to find it
What if you only have junk?
How to price items for sale
How/where to advertise/market - or -
      How to get the word out!
How to get MORE people to your sale!
How to set up your garage sale 'store'
How to prepare your stuff for sale
How to negotiate with buyers
How many people do you need to help you?
What about neighborhood (co-op) garage sales?
What to do with leftover merchandise
Condo Sales
So Your Moving...
Garage Sales for Fundraising
How to Cash In on Garage Sales!
Do's and Don'ts

...and so on.

So, let's get started!

WHY ARE GARAGE SALES SO POPULAR?

It is estimated that over 60,000,000 people in the United States go to garage sales each year! Why is that? For many reasons, but most importantly:

* Most garage sale customers go to the sales in order to find bargains; both to find a specific item (clothes, t.v. set, etc.), or to 'shop around', and see what they can find.

*There are some garage sale 'junkies' who do this for a hobby (or even a living), by looking for 'steals'. These people are more knowledgeable about antiques and valuables, and are looking for a 'diamond in the rough'. There have been hundreds of stories of people who unwittingly sell a valuable antique, baseball card, or other collectable for several dollars, without realizing what they had.

*A great many of the garage sale visitors are people who are just 'shopping', or passing the time. To many, this is a fun, pressure-free environment where people go to look through others' treasures, and if they find something they like, will proceed to bid on it. Where else can someone go shopping, and 'name their price'?

WHAT DO YOU SELL?

This is the simplest question to answer! You will be surprised at what you can sell, and what people will want to buy. Early on in our garage sale lives, we had dozens of pairs of shoes in bags that my wife stored in our crawl space. Before one of our sales, Mike suggested that we sell the shoes. Pam almost had a stroke over the thought, saying that no one would buy someone else's shoes! Boy, was she wrong! We'll never forget (since it's so rare) during the first day of the garage sale, when we had already sold over 20 pairs of shoes, that Pam turned to Mike with a look of amazement and *admitted that she was wrong! WOW!*

Anyway, so much for marital sarcasm. Other things that can be sold are:

clothing	books
appliances	furniture
lamps, fixtures	stamp collections
old computers, copiers	t.v.'s
pictures	rugs, carpet
bicycles, scooters	lawnmowers,

gardening tools
flowers, pots, vases   kitchen utensils
pots & pans, plates, silverware, cups, glasses, etc.
stereos, speakers
fish tanks   chairs, desks
old knick-knacks from Aunt Dorothy
shoes   sports equipment, and
                                        clothing
old bathroom scales   drapes, blinds
children's toys

...and so on.

Hopefully, you get the picture. You can sell *anything*, with a few exceptions. You should never sell anything illegal (firearms, drugs, etc.). Also, we don't feel right selling food to the customers, except under special circumstances that we will explain later.

I don't want any yes-men around me.
I want everybody to tell me the truth
even if it costs them their jobs.

Samuel Goldwyn

WHERE TO FIND IT

Garage sale stuff can be found just about anywhere. Another benefit of having a garage sale is that you usually handle 'spring cleaning' at the same time. While looking for garage sale merchandise, you will be going through your garage, attic, basement, crawl space, utility room, furnace room, storage shed, bedroom closets, under the bed, wherever you may store anything! While you are moving things around and checking out strange boxes and bags, you will effectively be straightening things up, without even thinking about it.

Another benefit of going through old boxes is that you may find something that you had lost several years ago! Every so often we'll come across something that we lost a long time ago.

Which items should go into the garage sale 'pile'? If you have bags or boxes that hadn't been opened for a year or two (or longer), then you obviously are not going to use the item. So why not turn it into money? We do! Our philosophy when sorting through things is; if we don't plan on using this in the near future, and don't see any reasonable rationale to hold on to it, then *why not turn it into cash?*

The great thing in this world
is not so much where we are,
but in what direction we are moving.

Oliver Wendell Holmes

WHAT IF YOU ONLY HAVE JUNK?

Or, where do you get enough saleable items for a successful garage sale? Good question. Let's assume that you follow the steps in this book, and you have a dynamite garage sale, with net proceeds after advertising of $3,000. Sound impossible? If you haven't had a garage sale (or house cleaning) for years or decades, this is a distinct possibility!

But now, this is the second year, and you don't have decades worth of 'stuff' stored in every nook and cranny of your home. How do you get enough stuff to make the garage sale interesting?

You need other sources for stuff. Always make a point to tell your friends, neighbors and family members (well in advance) that you are planning a garage sale. More often then not, they will respond that they have been trying to get rid of an old air conditioner that is just taking up room in their basement, or they are getting new furniture in their dining room, and want to get rid of their old furniture.

Once you have developed a reputation in the neighborhood that you have very successful and active garage sales, you may want to circulate a flyer in your neighbors' mailboxes, indicating that you are planning a sale, and they can 'consign' their items at your sale for a 20% charge. This means that they can bring their stuff over, already priced with their own tickets, and you can sell it for them, with you keeping 20% of each sale. This gives you some additional cash flow and traffic, and it allows your neighbors to sell stuff without advertising, or being stuck at home at their own garage sale. It is important that each neighbor/participant fill out a paper with a list of their items that they are bringing you, what their asking price for those items are (in case the price tags get lost), what they are willing to accept (so you know how much you can negotiate), and that you will receive a 20% 'commission' for selling their stuff.

How does this benefit you? Several ways. You would certainly not want to charge family members a percentage of the sale of their merchandise (although they may offer to pay for your advertising, or a small percentage for your troubles). However, neighbors and friends are a little different. You should have no problem charging them a 20% fee for selling their stuff, since you're spending the weekend stuck at home 'working' at the sale, moving around their stuff to make it fit inside your sales area, and negotiating with potential buyers, while they're playing golf, going to a sporting event, or otherwise having a great time.

Other than monetary, there are other benefits of getting other stuff when you don't have a lot to sell yourself. Remember, one of the most important factors of a successful garage sale is...

The more stuff you have, the more people will come!

If you are able to advertise to people that there will be hundreds of interesting items, including 25 pieces of furniture, hundreds of items of clothing, dozens of miscellaneous items, this will generate much more traffic than an ad that says that there will be a desk, two chairs and a wastepaper basket. The more stuff you have, the more people will come!

Other sources for 'stuff' includes:

*Going to other peoples' garage sales, flea markets, rummage sales, etc. and finding bargains for resale. If you are a serious garage sale marketer, you will be able to find things cheap enough at someone else's sale, to resell at your own. *Warning* - don't buy something for resale unless you are sure that you will be able to sell it right away! Otherwise, you may see that item go for less than you paid for it, or worse yet, in your garbage!

*You can buy some items in bulk at flea markets, close-out stores, or regular stores, and then split them up and sell the items individually for a profit! For example, tool chests can be bought in large packages at bargain prices. Many times, someone is only looking for one item, which you will sell them at a profit. How? Purchase a large kit for $9.99, and price the individual items at 99 cents. The kit may have 40 pieces, so even though you may not sell everything from the kit at this sale, you would only have to sell ten of the forty pieces to break even! And tools are one of the most popular items at garage sales.

Other examples of splitting bulk purchases include socks, craft items, office supplies (pencils, pens, paper, etc.), computer disks, blank video and audio tapes. The possibilities are endless!

I always wanted to be somebody,
but I should have been more specific.

Lily Tomlin

HOW TO PRICE ITEMS FOR SALE

This is the second hardest task that most people have to do while organizing their sale. How do you know if you're pricing you things too high, or too low? Remember, most of the things that you are selling at the sale are not only things that you have no use for, but in many cases after the sale, you may be leaving them at your curb for the garbage man, and not get a penny for them. Even worse, you may have to *pay* to have some items removed after the sale. Therefore, be sure to

Price each item to make sure that it sells!

Again, your goal is to make sure that you get rid of things, and you don't want the clutter any more. Therefore, just because Aunt Martha gave you that loveseat in 1973, and there is sentimental value attached, you can't get extra money for that sentimental value. Chances are, the buyer of that loveseat didn't even know Aunt Martha!

On the other hand, you don't want to price things too low. Just because your buyer didn't know Aunt Martha, that doesn't mean that they should pay $5.00 for the loveseat. So how do you price things?

There are different strategies for different classifications of items. For furniture, televisions, stereos, lamps, and other items of real value, we typically use this formula. Figure out in your mind what an item would cost a buyer new from a store. We then use, as a starting point, a 75% markdown. In other words, if Aunt Martha's loveseat would be sold in the store for $240.00 new, we would start out at $60.00 - $75.00. We figure that you want to price something at a value that the buyer can't match, and make it

An offer that the buyer can't refuse!

You should always assume that a buyer is intelligent, and knows value to a certain extent. Thus, he may know that, even on sale, that loveseat can be had *new* for around $200.00. Since buyers go to garage sales for bargains, you want to make *everything* at your sale seem like a bargain, because

If you price one item too high and the buyer knows it, he will think everything is priced too high!

On marginally valuable items, such as stereo systems and record players that may be out of date, with the new technology of cd systems, etc., you will want to price these items accordingly. If a stereo system cost you $250.00 new, you may want to start your price at $30.00 - $50.00. These are items that you are no longer using, you have no need for them, and there isn't a huge market to sell them anywhere else. Don't be afraid to sell something at a low price. What you may find out is, if you sell something to someone at a bargain, he may decide to look around more and purchase other things at the sale, since he feels that you are giving people great deals. He may, more often than not, buy something that you had no use for, and he has no use for either, because he can't pass up a bargain! More often than not, he may be selling that item next spring at his own garage sale!

What about items that have less perceived value, such as used shoes, clothing, cheap vases, trinkets, etc.? First of all, we don't sell clothing that is damaged (torn, stained etc.) unless we indicate so on a tag on the clothing. These items are marked down to almost nothing ($1.50 - $3.00). We usually sell used shoes and sandals for $2.50 a pair, and boy, you should see how fast they sell! Again, price these items that are 'worthless' to you cheap enough to make them your 'loss leaders', getting people in the door, and making them think that you have marked everything down to almost nothing!

If you are selling clothing, this is a little more difficult to price, since we could be talking about a wide variety of items. We try to hang more expensive outfits or suits on a rack, and these items are individually marked (usually anywhere from $5.00 - $20.00 depending upon the original value and the condition). Less expensive items such as shirts, slacks, etc. may be put on long folding tables that may have a sign such as: "$2.50 PER ITEM", or "$6.00 FOR ANY THREE ITEMS ON THIS TABLE".

The final point regarding pricing, is that, 95% of the time, people go to garage sales to negotiate. So, make sure that your asking price is not what you want to end up with. If you want $10.00 for a lamp, make the asking price $15.00. Chances are, your buyer will offer $5.00, and you will typically end up at $10.00, which is where you wanted to be. In other words, always give yourself some room to negotiate. A buyer will perceive that he has gotten even a better deal if he/she is able to talk you down on your price.

If you have many small items that must be priced individually, we recommend that you use masking tape with a black ink pen! This is the simplest and quickest way to get prices on your stuff, and masking tape will easily come off almost anything!

Drive thy business, or it will drive thee.

Benjamin Franklin

HOW TO ADVERTISE/MARKET
YOUR GARAGE SALE

Now that you know what you're selling, and you have an idea what you are selling everything for, you must ADVERTISE! If you don't let everyone know that you are conducting the SALE OF THE CENTURY, then your sale will not be successful, no matter how low you price everything.

Marketing comes in many forms, and takes some thought. Fortunately for you, we have made all the mistakes, tested numerous ideas over the years, and **you** have the great fortune to benefit from all of our mistakes over the past couple of decades. The first thing we will discuss is

WHEN TO CONDUCT THE GARAGE SALE

Since we are writing you from the northern midwest, we have four distinct seasons. Our strategy for every part of the country will still apply as follows. We obviously aren't going to conduct a garage sale during winter, cold or rainy periods. We want to have a garage sale during the optimum time when everyone will be glad to go outside and browse. In the northern part of the country, this would be summer time (well after the rainy season of April and May), and in southern climates, this would be during periods when people are most likely to venture outside. Check long-range weather reports for your area, or the almanac if you have no clue when to have a sale. The weather during the weekend is very important to the success of your sale!

Weather isn't the only thing to consider when you are trying to decide on a good weekend. A good strategy is to try to figure out when the majority of people get paid (usually around the 1st and 15th of the month), and schedule the sale around then. If people just got paid, and they haven't had time to pay their bills yet, they may be walking around with 'extra' money, and may be more willing to spend it at your sale.

Just as important - you don't want to schedule a sale around a holiday! Either a large portion of your potential customers may be out of town, they may have to entertain family from out of town, or they will be preoccupied with other 'holiday' matters! Schedule a weekend when there is nothing else of significance happening; that way you can be assured of a good crowd of buyers or lookers who have nothing else to do!

Now that we know which season to have the sale, let's narrow it down even further. We recommend a Friday - Sunday sale. Although some people only have their sale on Saturday and Sunday, we find that starting on Friday is very important, since you will be getting weekday and weekend people. Remember, you are shooting for the largest crowds possible! If you are not an experienced garage sale person, you will be surprised how many people show up before your garage opens its doors early Friday morning!

As far as the times, we usually run our sales from 9:00 a.m. until 5:30 p.m. on Friday and Saturday, and 9:00 a.m. until 4:00 p.m. on Sunday. This is not cut in stone, but as the day goes on, if you see a great deal of traffic showing up after 4:00 p.m. on your street, you may want to extend the time a little bit.

HOW/WHERE TO ADVERTISE

A garage sale without advertising/promotion will not be very successful. This has been proven again and again. Where do you advertise? We would suggest checking out the dominant daily newspapers in your community. Look for garage sale ads, and discover which ones have the most garage sale ads. If one paper has a great deal more ads than the other papers, advertise there! If there are 2 - 3 papers who all generate about the same amount of ads, advertise in all three. Garage sale 'junkies' (people who frequent many garage sales and buy) know which papers are best for garage sale ads. These are the papers that you want to advertise in.

Also, in addition to the dominant paper, if there is a local paper for your neighborhood or community, it wouldn't hurt to place an ad there as well. This is because you are getting a local readership, people won't have to travel as far, and the cost of the ad is usually much cheaper in a small, local paper.

Additionally, one of the best places to advertise is in a local advertiser, penny-saver or similar free weekly publication. This is because the advertising cost is typically cheaper, and many people who frequent garage sales look at these weekly shoppers for bargains.

What does the ad include? Generate traffic by showing the people that there are bargains that THEY will be interested in! You can do this by letting them know that there is TONS OF STUFF, and that it is priced right! Here is a sample ad that we used recently for one of our garage sales:

** GIGANTIC GARAGE SALE **
Multiple house sale has hundreds of
items! Must see to believe! 25
pieces of Furniture, 100's of
pieces of like-new clothing, 2 t.v.'s,
7 lamps, full set patio furniture, 100's
of misc. items - must see/must sell!
Fri - Sun 9-5 555 Main St. Chicago

Notice several important things. We say 'multiple house sale' even though the sale is only at your house. This is because we have items from other homes. We specified the large-ticket items to generate interest, we exhibited some urgency, we put the day and times and location of the sale. Abbreviations can work, but make sure that the average person will know what you are trying to abbreviate. Notice that we did not put the phone number. We don't want calls all hours of the day or night to answer questions about the type and manufacturer of the furniture, how old the t.v.'s are, etc. Putting your phone number in the ad will usually not help you make a sale!

If you are having a moving sale - please specify so! When you advertise in large letters MOVING SALE, this draws attention, and attracts more buyers and bargain hunters than anything else that you could imagine! However, don't advertise a moving sale, unless you really are moving!

When do you place the ad? I usually begin the day before the sale, on a Thursday, because that is a big shoppers' advertising day anyway, and will continue through Sunday. One Hint: My ad on Sunday may be a little different, since it's your last chance to sell your stuff! You may want to add catch lines such as "Last Day - Everything must Go!", or "Last Day - 25% off already low prices!", or "Every reasonable offer considered!". Remember, you are trying to generate *traffic*!

HOW TO ADVERTISE FOR FREE!

How would you like to get hundreds of dollars of advertising for **FREE**? Marketing geniuses all over the country will tell you that the most productive form of advertising is FREE ADVERTISING, which can be had by almost anyone, by using a little bit of ingenuity and creativity. Free advertising is generally in the form of general interest news releases, which are read by more people, and carry much more credibility, than a classified ad. Also, since your cost for the news release is **zero**, your return will be good regardless of the response!

Look in any newspaper or community paper, and you will see general interest stories about people, places or businesses, which is usually nothing more than some news that was sent into the publication by a savvy individual. Just think, if the newspaper has space to fill, and they receive something from you that will be of interest, then you have solved their problem for free! They won't have to pay writers to fill their space for them if they receive good articles from the public.

There is a good chance that you may have heard or read about this book, Garage Sale Magic, in a press release in a newspaper. What this is, is a news release that a newspaper, magazine or tabloid runs to fill up their paper, when they need some 'filler' space, and when they feel that the news release is newsworthy.

Who uses press releases? The obvious sources, such as newspapers, magazines, local readers, advertisers, etc. But don't ignore other avenues as well. Depending upon your situation, you could send your story to the church or other religious affiliation that you belong to (usually they have a monthly or quarterly newsletter), health club, a targeted retailer (depending upon the unique items that you have for sale), or any other place that prints a paper or newsletter for local distribution.

What would make a newsworthy story? Your creativity is the only limitation to what you can write about. Let's assume that you (and your ancestors) lived in the same home for over 100 years, and you have many antiques to sell. Send a news release which details the historical significance of the home, the family, and anything else that may have some interest to the average person reading that article. Remember,

**...if it isn't of interest to just about everyone,
it won't be printed!**

Another example would be to play a 'charity' angle. If you had a tragedy, and one of your family members lost his/her life due to cancer; you could donate 50% of the proceeds of the sale to Cancer Research, or another cancer related charitable organization. Many people would have sympathy for such a worthwhile cause.

What if you had some interesting items for sale that would be newsworthy? You could promote it as a UNIQUE garage sale, especially because you are selling many DIFFERENT items, including some valuable sports memorabilia, some furniture that was in a former president's home when he was a child, a litter of 12 kittens that will be looking for caring homes, a huge book collection that you accumulated over twenty years and must get rid of, unique hobby - type merchandise that you must liquidate, such as a coin or stamp collection, model airplanes, trains, cars, magazines, old pictures or painting of your community showing its early years, etc. But keep in mind, just mentioning a stamp collection won't get you in the paper. It must be a unique, huge, rare or valuable collection; something to pique interest!

Following is a sample press release. You can use the format of this release to send to the editorial department of the various publications (check your local yellow pages for all the newspapers to send it to). As far as when to send the release, remember to give it plenty of time for inclusion into your targeted publication. If it is a monthly publication, you must get it to them at least two weeks prior to their deadline for the issue that you need it in. If it is a daily newspaper that you are sending your information to, you must send the news release at least two weeks prior to the weekend of your sale. Another important tip is to make is seem more like a NEWS article, and less like advertising! Also, keep it short! The less editing that the paper has to do, the better chance it will have of getting selected to run.

****

Contact: Mike & Pam Williams
Phone # 123/356-0559

MAYBERRY, MN. - The Cancer Research Society will be getting an unexpected, but certainly welcome donation by Mike and Pam Williams of Mayberry in a couple of weeks. Mike and Pam recently lost their father to cancer, and have decided to arrange a garage sale in his honor. Thirty percent of their proceeds will go to the Cancer Research Society, which is a national organization that spends millions of dollars per year looking for a solution to one of society's deadliest killers.

This won't be just any garage sale! There will be items donated by dozens of neighbors and local businesses, and this is anticipated to be one of the largest single garage sales of the year! Every item will be sold at bargain prices, so you won't want to miss it.

The sale will be held the weekend of Fri. - Sun., June 3 - 5, at 135 Main Street in Mayberry. This is located two houses north of the intersection of Main and Checker streets. A big turnout is hoped for in support of this very worthwhile cause.

HOW TO GET MORE PEOPLE AT YOUR SALE!

Advertising is only one way to get the word out about your sale. There are other things that we always do, and they are just as important.

Signage. We always get plenty of garage sale signs to put at the corner of our block, at busy streets and intersections within several blocks of our home (either put your address with an arrow, or just a large arrow pointing to the direction of your home with the words TWO BLOCKS, or whatever the distance is), and make sure that people can logically follow the signs to your home! If it isn't easy, they will give up if they get lost. We ask neighbors/friends who live on corners or busy intersections if we can put signs at a visible point of their yard. These signs are put up the evening before the days of the sale.

In the event that you are selling merchandise for your neighbors, make sure to ask them to use their front yard for additional signage.

Another thing to write on the signs is YOUR ADDRESS! Why? You have invested lots of money in the signs, and would like to use them over and over again. Before we started putting our address on the signs, we would find them missing from different parts of the neighborhood! Other people with a planned sale would 'borrow' our signs for their own sale. However, with our address clearly printed on the signs in **dark black ink**, the signs were only good for *our* sale, and became undesirable to others.

Index cards. Get 3 X 5 index cards with the script from your advertising, and post them on bulletin boards at all busy retail establishments, including supermarkets, department stores, ice cream parlors, fast food restaurants, churches, etc. Use magic marker, colored index cards, and make every word easy to read and understand! Include directions or distance from the location of the index card (three blocks south on Main Street; one block west of the McDonalds, etc.).

Make your sale easy to find!

Signs/Posters. Get cardboard or regular copy paper, write your ad with directions, and tape them onto the inside of glass windows/doors of busy stores (with permission, of course). Tell the store manager that you will promptly remove your sign the day after the sale.

SPECIAL HINT: Try to use a 'goldenrod' colored background for all signs, posters and posted notices, with black print or marker. This color combination stands out better than any other, and is easier to read (ask any sign expert!).

Banners. Check the local yellow pages to find a store that sells banners, or a string of flags. Nothing attracts drivers' eyes more than colorful banners or flags that are waiving in the wind, which are spread out across your front yard, attached to trees, your house, whatever else you can attach it to (How many car dealers DON'T have banners?). Make sure that the banners are attached high enough to not interfere with your shoppers' walking, but low enough for easy visibility (we use about 8 feet as a general rule, depending upon what we can attach them to). We have over 100 feet of multi-colored banners on a vinyl string, which cost us less than $20.00, and can be used over and over again for years!

If you don't have banners, then put up a United States flag, or anything else that will cause people to look in your direction! These 'distractions' will bring more people to your sale.

Now for some creativity! Remember, your goal is to get as many drivers (and walkers) to stop and see what you have as possible! How about a lemonade stand near the front of your garage sale, manned by your child, or a neighbor's child, offering FREE LEMONADE! You won't spend more than $5.00 for the whole weekend for lemonade mix, and the additional traffic you generate will make it worthwhile! Also, your lemonade person can help you keep an eye on things when crowds come. A neighbor, who happens to be a great cook, once made dozens of HOME-MADE EGGROLLS! She charged $.50 per egg roll to cover her costs, but <u>boy, did we get traffic</u>!

Parking. Make sure there is plenty of convenient parking in front of your home. Park your car(s) far enough away that they won't take up valuable parking, and ask your neighbors if they could help by doing the same (if they usually park on the street). If there is not convenient parking, many people may keep on going, even if they slowed down, and saw something of interest. Remember to park your own cars down the block, so you don't take up valuable customer parking spaces!

Never keep up with the Joneses.
Drag them down to your level.
It's cheaper.

Quentin Crisp

HOW TO SET UP YOUR GARAGE SALE 'STORE'

This is a good time to talk about the best way to set up your 'store', since you are trying to maximize your customer base by having people stop and look. The night before, you will have tagged everything possible with a price, since you will be too busy to answer everyone's questions about items that aren't priced the days of the sale. Everything will be piled into the garage, or close to the front door if your sale will be in your front yard (if you don't have a garage).

You will want to have your stuff spread out as much as possible, for maximum visibility, ease of walking around things, and to give the appearance of organization and to let people see that you have enough items to make their stopping worthwhile! Put your most desirable items (lighter furniture pieces, clothing on racks, etc.) in your front yard.

Don't hide your best merchandise in your garage!

Make sure that people can see as much as they can from their car! Spread out your shoes on a blanket in your front yard.

Spread out children's toys and games on other blankets, so kids can see them and play with them! In other words, spread things out!

The only items that should be left in the garage are the larger furniture pieces that will be difficult to move in and out every day, and pictures that you may have put on the garage walls, as well as heavy items. If a driver sees banners at your house with hundreds of items strewn all over your front yard, with people milling around, chances are he/she will want to stop and check things out.

If you have lots of clothing, you have two options. We like to rent or borrow a couple of racks, and hang whatever is hangable. This makes it easier for buyers to look through things, and less mess. You should also have some long folding tables where you can put piles of clothing for people to look at conveniently.

Make sure that all electrical items for sale are nearby a plug or extension cord, so people can turn them on to make sure that they work. This takes lots of the perceived risk out of buying the item, and people will spend more money if they feel that you are being honest with them about each item. You should not sell any items that don't work, unless there is a sign to that effect on the item, specifying that the item doesn't work, that they are buying the item 'as is', and that the cheap price reflects the condition of the item. You are much better off not having an argument later on because an item didn't work, after the buyer thought that it did.

On the same vein, it is a nice touch to have some of the electrical items 'on' during the sale. Why not have a radio playing, or the stereo or t.v. playing that you are trying to sell? After all, not only does it bring attention to the item, but is shows your buyers that the item is in good working condition.

HOW TO PREPARE YOUR STUFF FOR SALE

Such a simple idea that so many people don't follow in order to maximize your sale price is to

Make your stuff look good

Simply put, clean and dust whatever items you can to make things look better. If items look 'like new', then someone will pay more for them. If items are dusty, dirty or look like you didn't care enough to take care of the item, it will look like garbage, and buyers will pay you accordingly.

If you have furniture that is to be sold, clean and polish it before you put it outside at the sale. The first impression of the item that you are selling is lasting, and it will affect the sales price, not to mention your ability to sell it at all!

Where you place the stuff is just as important! Inevitably you may have miscellaneous items in the yard on your grassy areas. Make sure that they are placed on a blanket, tarp, plastic or some other protective 'shield' from the grass stains, damp grass, or mud. This makes keeping your goods clean that much easier!

The best way to keep your word
is not to give it.

Napoleon Bonaparte

HOW TO NEGOTIATE WITH BUYERS

Many people tend to shy away from running garage sales because they don't have the confidence or willingness to negotiate with buyers. We find that, if you have the right approach, negotiations rarely become antagonistic, and it is always just a friendly exchange.

One of the most important keys in your negotiation, as we discussed earlier, is in your asking price. Always give yourself some room to come down, since

95% of garage sale buyers will want to talk you down to their price!

Using the example of the lamp that we discussed before, you are asking $15.00 (knowing that you want to end up with $10.00). An astute, experienced buyer will offer you $5.00, and you will just shake your head and squirm, insisting that this lamp cost you $40.00 when you bought it new, plus tax. After some friendly discussion (always keep it friendly, with a smile on your face, since you *want* him to own that lamp), you decide to split the difference with him, and settle on $10.00, even though you were looking to get $12.50. Most reasonable buyers will agree to split the difference with you, which sounds like a fair compromise!

Negotiation must appear to be a win-win situation for you and the buyer!

If the buyer does not feel like he is getting a bargain, he will most likely not buy from you. Try to be as forthcoming as possible with information. Plug in the lamp to show him that it works, and tell him that you have 'tested' the lamp for three years to make sure that it works, before selling it to him.

Using a sense of humor can disarm a tough buyer - don't take the negotiation too seriously!

Successful negotiation, which involves some give and take on both sides, results in successful garage sales. An important benefit of developing a reputation over the years of successful garage sales *is* the reputation that you develop! This may sound silly, but each spring we get approached by friends who ask us when our next garage sale will be, and to remember to call them ahead of time! Some of them are looking to participate with some of their stuff, and others want an early *preview* to see what we will be selling!

Occasionally you will get a buyer who starts developing a pile of things to buy. Although he will attempt to negotiate each item down to its lowest price, this procedure can take forever! It is recommended that you note that your purchaser will have lots of items to purchase, and that you will make a better deal for him once he is done shopping.

Once the pile is complete, add up the asking price of each item, and then take 20% off of the top. This solves the headache of negotiating on each item. Invariably, the purchaser will suggest a discount that will approach 30 - 35%, and you can settle on a 25% discount, since he is 'such a good customer'. It is our experience that, unless the purchaser is just plain unreasonable to begin with, you will be able to work out a 'bulk' sale as we just described.

HOW MANY PEOPLE DO YOU NEED TO HELP YOU?

This is a touchy question without a clear answer. During the three days of the garage sale, there will be busy times and slow times. The busiest times are typically early in the morning when the garage sale first opens up. You will find that if you have advertised properly, both in the paper, and with strategically placed signs throughout the neighborhood, and your banners are up, there will be a bunch of people waiting in their cars before the doors open.

Keep in mind that, when the doors open, you will need at least 15 minutes to place things out on the yard, move furniture or clothing tables onto the driveway, and organize the garage. You can't do all of this alone. It is best to have 1 - 2 helpers first thing each morning.

After the first hour or two, when things settle down to a steady stream of customers, you don't need as much help. It is recommended that you have at least one helper at all times. Since you have stuff all over the place, it is difficult for you to concentrate on handling customers and taking their money, as well as keeping an eye on what is going on in the front yard. Remember, four eyes are better than two!

What about before the sale? Keep in mind that there is plenty of preparation ahead of time before the sale. You need to plan for all of the signage, banners, advertising, etc. You also need to plan for the pricing (and marking) of the items in some form. Don't underestimate the time that this will take! It is not uncommon for us to be pricing the items in the garage, the night before the first day of the sale, until after midnight. Planning a-head can make a big difference - you will need plenty of rest once the sale day begins!

I like long walks,
especially when they are taken
by people who annoy me.

Fred Allen

WHAT ABOUT NEIGHBORHOOD (JOINT) GARAGE SALES?

Our neighborhood typically has a joint garage sale, when there are 15 - 20 homes participating. This is a good idea from the standpoint that all the homes share in the cost of advertising and promotion, and a lot of traffic is generated.

We never participate in neighborhood garage sales for a very simple reason. We believe that, for the small amount of money that we spend on advertising; typically less than $150.00, we are not saving much money with the joint advertising and promotion. We feel that we can generate plenty of interest and traffic with our sale. The garage sale buyers only have so much to spend when they visit garage sales over the weekend, and *we don't want to compete with 15 other homes in the same neighborhood for the buyers' dollars!* You want the buyers to concentrate on your sale, your stuff, and don't want them to have an excuse to leave your sale to visit the garage down the block that also has bargains. If someone sees your sign or your ad in the paper, they are coming to see your stuff, and *to buy your stuff!*

WHAT TO DO WITH LEFTOVER MERCHANDISE

At the end of the three day marathon, after you have cleaned out your house and sold thousands of dollars of stuff, you realize that there is still some left! This will happen - it is rare that *everything* will sell at any sale. However, some careful planning will limit the leftovers.

Step one. If you have lots of furniture and you have advertised properly, chances are you will be visited by some second-hand furniture retailers, who are happy to take the furniture off you hands for 10 - 20 cents on the dollar. If they come in the first or second day of your sale, take their business card, and let them know that you will contact them if you haven't sold all the furniture. If they haven't showed up, then contact them first thing Monday, and tell them to bring cash. These people are anxious for bargains!

Step two. By Sunday, you will have evaluated what you have left over, and will be much more flexible on your pricing. We usually see some of the same people on Sunday that we saw on Friday, because they didn't buy that lamp on Friday, but they really wanted it. Although they wanted to pay $7.50 and you were holding out for $10.00, you may want to negotiate further on Sunday, and try to get $8.50 or so for it. As a last resort, you may as well sell it for $7.50 if that is all your buyer wants to pay. Taking $7.50 now is preferable to storing it in the house again another year until the next garage sale, and there is no guarantee that it'll sell then! Although we continue to use the 'lamp' example, this applies for furniture, clothing, whatever you're trying to sell! Your goal is to get rid of the stuff as soon as possible, and turn that 'junk' into cash!

Step three. By the same token, if you have not been able to negotiate an acceptable price for a certain item with a buyer during the weekend, take down his name and phone number, and note the item. Indicate to him that, if it doesn't sell by Sunday, you will be glad to give him a call after the sale, and sell it to him at his price. Keep in mind that, although this is a last-ditch effort to sell that item, the buyer *may* have changed his mind after thinking about it, and decided not to buy it after all. But that is always the chance that you are taking when you don't sell the item right away!

Step four. Contact Salvation Army or other charitable organizations in your area. These establishments will come around with their own truck, give you a receipt for what they took, and haul it away for free! That receipt is very important! Usually there is an estimated dollar value for each item. You are able to receive a tax deduction for these items as a charitable contribution! Thus, you can make money from your leftover garage sale items at no cost to you! Charities will usually take furniture, clothes in good condition, appliances and stereos as long as they work - anything that they reasonably think that they can resell.

Step five. Even after you have had a very successful garage sale, and taken care of steps one through four, you may still have some junk left. Chances are, much of the leftovers is junk, and won't sell at the next garage sale next year! Look through each item. If you reasonably believe that it won't ever sell, and you have no further use for it - throw it out! Don't take up valuable storage room and house space for junk! If, by some strange fluke, you have some valuable leftover items, then save them for your next garage sale.

CONDO/APARTMENT SALES

Garage sales don't have to be limited to those who live in single family homes. On the contrary, most of us live in apartments or condo buildings. As you know, there is less storage room available in apartments, so the need to get rid of excess 'stuff' is even more critically important! And having the ability to collect cash for that stuff makes it all the more worthwhile!

Getting started is as easy as posting a flyer in the lobby of the building in which you live, or distributing it to your neighbors in the building. Once you have worked out the details with your neighbors, and everyone is in agreement as to the dates, everyones' responsibilities, etc., then the rest is easy. By following the details of what has been learned in this book, you will be able to have a tremendous outpouring of excitement, since this will be a multiple home sale; and if each of your neighbors take the time to invite their friends and families to participate by bringing additional stuff to the sale, then these events can be extremely exciting, and you can expect big turnouts. Most important, is that you should not skimp on the advertising! You can split the cost over many households! Let people know that you are preparing a special event, and *they will come!*

SO YOU'RE MOVING...

If you're planning on selling your home, or even moving from your apartment, a garage sale is essential! There are so many great reasons to have a garage sale, with the most important being...

1. MONEY

When a family is planning a move, *money* is the biggest worry. A family who is moving (whether by selling their home or moving from a rental) is always in need of extra money. Sellers need money to fix up the home before they can sell it to maximize their price, and to pay for advertising (or list with a broker). Renters need money to fix up their apartment, find another apartment or put cash down on their first home, or to use it as a security deposit for their next rental. Both sellers and renters need money to pay for a mover, if they go that route.

2. GETTING RID OF UNWANTED JUNK

Regardless of your method of moving, one of the most important and least remembered strategies is to

get rid of whatever junk you don't need!

Why? Most people, when planning a move, concentrate so much on packing, that they don't realize that they can make a move much easier if their load is lightened! When you are preparing for the move, and starting to pack; that is when you will be handling everything in your home. Most people are amazed by the accumulation of stuff that has occurred over time! As you are holding each item, ask yourself:

...will I need these furnishings where I am moving to? If not, put it aside in a designated area for a sale!

...is this item worth to me what I can sell it for at a garage sale? If you don't sell it, then you have effectively paid that price for the item! For instance, if you have a lamp in storage that you haven't used in five years, and can get $10.00 for it - decide whether it's worth the $10.00 to you to keep it! Since you haven't used it in five years, chances are you have better use for the $10.00 CASH than you have for the lamp!

Will I be needing these items in the future (if you haven't used something; ie. a lamp, telephone, old clothing, ladder, your old dish set, an outdated stereo, an old typewriter, etc., or have lots of boxes full of 'junk' in storage, garage, crawl space, etc.)?

You will find that it's surprisingly easy to get rid of things that you will never need once you begin the process!

The most important thing is for you to decide once and for all, to make up your mind that these items are only taking up space, and should be gotten rid of!

If we haven't convinced you yet - answer this question: When moving, do you plan on filling your boxes with **garbage**? Probably not! That makes our advise even more compelling. Not only would you not make the effort to transfer your garbage to your new, clean abode, but you can't sell your garbage for **cash**! You will find dozens of items in your house that will not pass the above tests, and will be great candidates for you to sell at a garage sale!

Once you have put aside your 'sale' items, you will be free to pack everything else. Notice how much room you have saved in your moving vehicles, by leaving the junk behind! Recognize how much extra room you have in your new home, because you left the junk behind! Your moving time may be shortened significantly, because you will have made fewer trips to your new home. A basic rule of moving is:

Don't handle anything more often than absolutely necessary!

If you leave your junk behind, and pocket the cash instead, you will indeed have made the most important moving decision of all!

You've got to be very careful
if you don't know where you are going,
because you might not get there.

Yogi Berra

GARAGE SALES AND FUNDRAISING

Are you a member of a church, Rotary Club, Kiwanis, or would you like to help the American Cancer Society, Salvation Army or some other charitable organization? If so, garage sales (sometimes called 'rummage sales') can be the most powerful fundraising avenues available! By now, you have discovered some of the secrets of implementing a successful garage sale at your home. How is it different if done as an organization (church, charity, etc.)?

Fundraising makes garage sales most exciting for us, and we can't believe the response that we get when preparing for a fundraiser! The best way to illustrate this might be by example:

Let us take the example of a church not far from where we live which has suffered a loss, and the local newspaper mentions that the church may not be able to keep its doors open without some financial help. Although you had never been involved in such a large undertaking, you could come up with the idea that, if your garage sales could do so well, couldn't a church, with such a following, and the assistance from the local community, accomplish their goals as well?

There are many events that have been held over time to raise money for all types of special events and purposes - bake sales, raffles, bingo games; but we feel that a garage sale would be the best for several reasons. First, raffles, bingo and other games of chance have a limited number of winners, and plenty of losers; at bake sales, there is always the chance that someone may buy some cookies, cakes or donuts that don't taste good, could have foreign ingredients included, or is just plain FATTENING!

At a garage sale, everyone wins! Participants who bring their 'stuff' to an event get a chance to clean their house, and get to treat the donation as a charitable contribution.

By bringing this idea up to some of the membership, before you know it, you will be 'volunteered' to organize the 'garage sale'! How will you do it?

First, plan on a specific weekend to have the sale, which will be well in advance (4-5 weeks). Next, develop a one page summary of the event, including the dates, times, and most important, that merchandise will be needed from members of the church, their family, friends and neighbors. A sample of the memorandum follows:

****

COMMUNITY GARAGE SALE!

Friends - your help is needed!

Please join us for what will be the largest garage sale in town, and will be held the weekend of August 1, 1990.

If you have any items which you were planning on getting rid of (furniture, appliances, stereos, t.v.'s, lamps, clothing, couches, tables, chairs, desks, typewriters, old computers, stereo equipment, shoes, umbrellas, pictures, paintings, books, antiques, toys, games, pianos, etc.), please bring them to the ...

First Community Church
1434 First Avenue (across the street from the Kmart)
Thursday, August 3rd - Sunday, August 6th; from 9 - 5!

Volunteers will be needed to help with the garage sale - setup, delivery, sales and housekeeping help will be appreciated!

Your donation will be tax deductible* as a charitable contribution.
Come to the office for particulars, or call (555) 545-4411.

*See your accountant or advisor as to the deductibility of your contribution -
your tax situation may be unique.

You would treat this garage sale, or 'community sale' similar to a paper drive, which was popular for money-raising years ago in smaller communities. What happened there?

Schools would sponsor a paper drive about a month in advance, whereby the kids would inform their parents, relatives and neighbors to keep all of their newspapers in one pile, until shortly before the sale. At that time, the kids would come with their wagons, (or more often the parents in their cars, pick-up trucks or station wagons), make the rounds and pick all the piles of newspaper. It would then be taken to the school, where it would be weighed, and the children with the most tonnage would receive some award or other recognition. Then, large trucks would pick up the newspaper from the school, pay the school by the ton, and recycle it.

You can use the same basic formula for the community garage sale. Church members and their friends and relatives would all be made aware of the upcoming sale. They would distribute flyers as seen in the above example all around the community, and generate interest in the upcoming sale, while looking for volunteers to handle the necessities, including the preparation for the garage sale, setting up the merchandise (including pricing, cleaning, etc.), signage, posting notices all over town, someone to handle the donation slips as people brought stuff in, the actual sales force to handle three days of the sale, and so on.

Just like the paper drives of old, many people would go to neighbors for items for the community sale, as it is called, so they could accumulate large amounts of stuff, and therefore get 'credit' for bringing it in. Some of the more enterprising volunteers could go to repair shops for used and outdated typewriters, t.v. sets and stereo systems, and come back with quite a hall!

Businesses even contribute in a big way! Although a newspaper can't give away advertising for free, they can place several strategic articles (press releases) about the impending sale during the month of preparation, which would be worth thousands of dollars in free press! Several businesses would volunteer their trucks and drivers to pick up larger items (furniture, etc.) from people who couldn't otherwise arrange to have it delivered. Signs can be donated by hardware stores and sign companies, and many more property owners could give permission to have the signs displayed on their lawn during the three day event. And what an event!

Such an event can generate hundreds of donations, dozens of volunteers, and caused as much excitement as a circus! But the best part about it is the results! A well-run sale can bring in tens of thousands of dollars to the church, and everyone seems to get what they want! The community spirit would flourish, and a special spirit of 'goodwill' permeates the neighborhood.

These type of events, after they are successful, could be run annually for various worthwhile and needy charitable or philanthropic organizations in the neighborhood. After the first time, it becomes easier to coordinate, and many of the lose ends seem to fall into place much easier.

**Work done with little effort
is likely to yield little result.**

B.C. Forbes

HOW TO CASH IN ON GARAGE SALES!

As you have learned, garage sales run properly can not only be fun, but profitable as well! How would you like to cash in on this great money-making opportunity on a part - time or full - time basis? It's easier than you think!

Once you have had several successful garage sales, you will have begun to develop a reputation for being able to sell other peoples' merchandise. By keeping a list of those people, you are developing a list of 'suppliers' for your future sales.

Once you have decided to jump into the garage sale business (either full or part time), you can distribute flyers at your own garage sales, offering various related services, such as consulting for someone else's garage sales, being responsible for their signs, posters, advertising, etc., or just selling their merchandise at one of your sales for a specified fee (as discussed previously).

How would you like to prepare a garage sale each month? Depending on the part of the country in which you live, this may be tricky, but not impossible! If you live in a warm - climate state, you don't have to worry, but what if you live in the snow belt, where the winter winds whistle through your bones just when you're running outside for 30 seconds to get the newspaper? For those uninhabitable months that you can't spend outside, could you find an inside location to handle the sale for the weekend? How about a vacant storefront at a nearby shopping center? All you have to do is to contact the leasing agent, and ask them if you could use the storefront for the 3-4 days of your sale, and you will be happy to give them 5 - 10% of the expected receipts - IN CASH - IN ADVANCE! Many property owners with vacant stores would like to receive some additional cash to spend. An added benefit to the property owner is that you will be bringing additional traffic into their shopping center for that weekend, which will make the other merchants happy, and possibly draw attention to the vacant storefront.

You have many benefits as well. You will be able to stage a monthly garage sale (regardless of the weather); by holding it at a shopping center, you will have the benefit of a 'retail' location with additional exposure for your sale; and since most shopping centers are located at main thoroughfares, your signage will be seen by more potential customers than if you just had the sale at your home in a residential neighborhood.

But that's just the beginning. As a garage sale consultant, you could send sales letters to fundraising organizations, as discussed above. You could coordinate and arrange the whole sale for a set fee, or a percentage of the receipts.

You could advertise in the garage sale section of the local classified ads that you coordinate and prepare the whole garage sale for those who don't have the time, or inclination to do it themselves. Your initial consultation with them will help you decide if it will be worthwhile for you and for your potential client.

DO'S AND DON'TS

There are a few important things to consider when planning and implementing a garage sale, that needs extra emphasis:

Move your cars down the block.

Make sure that there is plenty of convenient parking for your customers. Some potential customers, if there isn't a convenient spot in front of your yard, will not make the effort to walk the additional fifteen steps to check out your stuff! Leave the best parking for your customers!

Have plenty of change on hand at the sale!

Sales can be lost if you don't have correct change! Make sure that you start each day with at least 20 - $1 bills; 5 - $5 bills; 3 - $10 bills, 20 - nickels, 20 - dimes and 20 - quarters. Pennies aren't important, since you aren't charging sales tax, and your total shouldn't require pennies.

Only take cash or money orders from your buyers.

NEVER take personal checks! The risk is too great. It is easier, if the buyer wants to buy from you, to ask them to get a money order from a nearby supermarket. You don't want collection risks - you want to keep things simple! We have had people who want to write a check say they live in the same neighborhood only two blocks away, and they only have a check. Even then, we don't waiver on this policy! The beauty of garage sales is that it is a cash business - there are no collection problems, lawyers, or headaches.

Treat each customer with respect - word of mouth is very important!

During the course of our garage sales, we enjoy hearing from a number of people that they will tell their brother or friend about the sale, since they need a couch or desk. Even more gratifying is when a buyer actually pays for an item, and then says that he heard about our sale from a friend of his. This means that we have treated people right!

Don't smoke during a garage sale!

Treat your visitors (customers) with respect. Observe that the majority of them do not like being subjected to second - hand smoke, and, by the same token, will be turned off by clothing or other items for sale that smells like smoke.

Clean up your yard (and your neighbors') after each sale!

You want to be a good neighbor. With all the traffic you are generating, there may be additional trash! When you close up each night, check your neighbors' yard, and make sure that none of your junk/trash has blown over to their yard.

Make sure your 'customers' park properly.

If your customers park in your neighbors' driveway, block their driveway, or double park on the street, it is your responsibility to tactfully ask them to move to a different parking space. Even if the customer gets irritated and leaves, your relationship with your neighbors is much more important. Chances are, if the customer gets upset by your asking him to move his car which was inconsiderately parked in the first place, you probably have not lost a sale!

Don't forget to pick up all of the neighborhood signs you have posted.

These signs are your sales tools that can be used year after year, as well as your banner! Store all these items in an easy - to - remember place, so you won't have to go to the time and expense to prepare new signs for your next sale!

Next time you see your neighbors, thank them for their patience.

Some neighbors may be upset with all the traffic you generated during the weekend, or the inconvenience that your sale caused. In either case, the next time you see them, tell them that you appreciate their patience, since they had to put up with the increased traffic and parkers.

Use some of your 'found' money to treat yourself - you deserve it!

Although you may want to use some of your money to pay off a credit card, or other important bills, put aside a chunk of that money to buy something for yourself that you wanted! Get that new refrigerator, a painting for the living room, a down payment for a car, or better yet -

take that summer vacation!

IF YOU'RE READING SOMEONE ELSE'S BOOK...
you may want your own!

If you have enjoyed this book, and feel that the information was useful, please use the coupon below to order copies for yourself, your friends, neighbors, employees, relatives, or anyone else who you think can use the invaluable tips delivered in Garage Sale Magic.

Please order today! *For Fastest Service, call 24 hours*
1-800-717-0770

Special Bulk Copy Discount Schedule

1 book - $13.45	10 books - $100.00
2 books- $24.00	20 books - $180.00
3 books- $36.00	50 books - $400.00
4 books- $48.00	100 books - $725.00
5 books- $59.00	Larger orders - please contact us!

All prices include both shipping and handling.

FREEDOM PUBLISHING COMPANY
400 West Dundee Road - Buffalo Grove, Il. 60089 (312)654-1775
Yes! Please send me _____ copies of the paperback edition of Garage Sale Magic. Enclosed is my check or money order for $_____, or please charge my__ Mastercard __ Visa __ American Express__Discover
No. _____ Exp. Date _____
Signature _____ Name _____
Address _____
City _____ State ___ Zip _____
Illinois residents please add 7% sales tax. Your order will be shipped within 24 hours!

IF YOU'RE READING SOMEONE ELSE'S BOOK...
you may want your own!

If you have enjoyed this book, and feel that the information was useful, please use the coupon below to order copies for yourself, your friends, neighbors, employees, relatives, or anyone else who you think can use the invaluable tips delivered in Garage Sale Magic.

Please order today! *For Fastest Service, call 24 hours*
1-800-717-0770

Special Bulk Copy Discount Schedule

1 book - $13.45	10 books - $100.00
2 books- $24.00	20 books - $180.00
3 books- $36.00	50 books - $400.00
4 books- $48.00	100 books - $725.00
5 books- $59.00	Larger orders - please contact us!

All prices include both shipping and handling.

FREEDOM PUBLISHING COMPANY
400 West Dundee Road - Buffalo Grove, Il. 60089 (312)654-1775
Yes! Please send me _____ copies of the paperback edition of Garage Sale Magic. Enclosed is my check or money order for $_____, or please charge my__ Mastercard __ Visa __ American Express__Discover
No. _____ Exp. Date _____
Signature _____ Name _____
Address _____
City _____ State ___ Zip _____
Illinois residents please add 7% sales tax. Your order will be shipped within 24 hours!
